POCKET MANUAL

Teams and players, facts and figures

WORLD FOOTBALL STARS

Published in October 2013

British Library Cataloguing-in-Publication Data:
A catalogue record for this book is available from
the British Library

ISBN 978 0 85733 504 3

Published by Haynes Publishing,
Sparkford, Yeovil, Somerset BA22 7JJ, UK
Tel: 01963 442030 Fax: 01963 440001
Int. tel: +44 1963 442030 Int. fax: +44 1963 440001
Email: sales@haynes.co.uk
Website: www.haynes.co.uk

Haynes North America, Inc.,
861 Lawrence Drive, Newbury Park
California 91320, USA

Design and layout by Richard Parsons

Photographs courtesy of Getty Images
(PA Photos used on pages 11, 35, 41, 57, 97 and 125)

All statistics and dates correct as of 14 July 2013

Printed in the USA by Odcombe Press LP,
1299, Bridgestone Parkway, La Vergne, TN 37086

The Author

This is the fifth book Nick Judd and Tim Dykes have produced together.
Nick has given up hope of seeing any Swindon Town players appear in these
pages. Southampton fan Tim is more hopeful.

POCKET MANUAL

Teams and players, facts and figures

WORLD FOOTBALL STARS

WORLD FOOTBALL STARS
CONTENTS

GLOBAL GATHERING

Europe and South America are footballing hotbeds that continue to supply a lot of the world's most exciting and talented players. Spain and Germany lead the way: 2014 World Cup finalists, perhaps?

BY POSITION	
Goalkeepers	3
Defenders	10
Midfielders	31
Forwards	16

Colombia — ②

Ivory Coast — ①

④ — Brazil

Chile — ①

② — Uruguay

④ — Argentina

Spain	⑫	**Uruguay**	②
Germany	⑨	**Wales**	②
Italy	⑥	**Chile**	①
Argentina	④	**Denmark**	①
Brazil	④	**Ivory Coast**	①
France	③	**Poland**	①
Holland	③	**Portugal**	①
Belgium	②	**Serbia**	①
Colombia	②	**Slovakia**	①
England	③	**Sweden**	①

SERGIO AGÜERO

DOB:	02.06.1988
POSITION:	Forward
HEIGHT:	172cm
WEIGHT:	74kg

ARGENTINA

Caps	45
Goals	18

CLUB CAREER

Games	293
Goals	133
Current club	**Manchester City**

Sixteen goals in 2012-13 represented a decent return for Argentina international Agüero, although his efforts couldn't quite match the epic standards he set the previous year. 'Kun' wrote himself into Manchester City folklore when he scored a sensational injury-time winner – his 30th goal of the season – on the last day to end the club's 44-year wait for the league title. At previous club Atlético Madrid, who he had joined for a then record fee of £15.75million, Agüero scored 91 goals in five seasons and won the Europa League in 2010. He has a low centre of gravity and is lethal inside the box.

XABI ALONSO

DOB:	**25.11.1981**
POSITION:	**Midfield**
HEIGHT:	**183cm**
WEIGHT:	**75kg**

SPAIN

Caps	107
Goals	15

CLUB CAREER

Games	405
Goals	27
Current club	**Real Madrid**

Stylish midfielder Alonso feels his role is simply to move the ball around the pitch, "from back to front and left to right." He must surely be considered one of the best at providing a seamless link between defence and attack, for few players read the game as well as him. Not surprisingly, football runs in Alonso's DNA. His father Periko won two La Liga titles with Real Sociedad, the club who gave Alonso junior his top-flight debut. The Spaniard has won a World Cup, two European Championship titles, the Champions League, FA Cup, Copa del Rey and La Liga.

DANI ALVES

DOB:	06.05.1983
POSITION:	Defence
HEIGHT:	171cm
WEIGHT:	64kg

BRAZIL

Caps	69
Goals	5

CLUB CAREER

Games	360
Goals	24
Current club	FC Barcelona

The role of the full-back is constantly evolving and Brazilian Dani Alves continues to set the standard. Few players boast his ability at both ends of the pitch. For example, in April 2013, he left fans, opponents and commentators open-mouthed with a sensational long-range assist using the outside of his boot in Barcelona's 2-2 draw with Paris St Germain in the Champions League. Assists come naturally to the 30-year-old. He contributed seven in 2012-13 as Barca won a 22nd La Liga title, 70 since joining the club in 2008. His overlapping runs and tenacity breaking forward are as important as his defensive capabilities.

GARETH
BALE

DOB:	**16.07.1989**
POSITION:	**Midfield**
HEIGHT:	**183cm**
WEIGHT:	**74kg**

WALES

Caps	41
Goals	11

CLUB CAREER

Games	186
Goals	47
Current club	**Tottenham Hotspur**

The departures of Luka Modric (Real Madrid) and Rafael van der Vaart (Hamburg) in the summer of 2012 enabled Bale to take centre stage at Tottenham Hotspur. He certainly seized the opportunity, starting the new campaign with a superb goal that earned Spurs a first win at Old Trafford in 23 years. His pace, ability to ride challenges and willingness to shoot from distance proved a constant source of goals, racking up 21 in 33 league games. In May, he was awarded both the PFA Player's Player of the Year and Football Writers' Player of the Year awards.

KARIM BENZEMA

DOB:	17.12.1987
POSITION:	Forward
HEIGHT:	183cm
WEIGHT:	73kg

FRANCE

Caps	58
Goals	15

CLUB CAREER

Games	236
Goals	98
Current club	**Real Madrid**

French international Benzema is a strong, two-footed striker with a predatory eye for goal. He is four years into a six-year contract at Real Madrid but his recent form – and the departure of Jose Mourinho – find him linked with a move away from the Bernabéu. He faced fierce competition from Gonzalo Higuain for a starting place in 2012-13 but scored 20 goals 33 games in all competitions. The previous season, Benzema notched a career-high 21 league goals in what was a record-breaking campaign: Madrid scored 121 goals (with a goal difference of +89) before lifting their 32nd La Liga title.

GIANLUIGI BUFFON

DOB:	28.01.1978
POSITION:	Goalkeeper
HEIGHT:	190cm
WEIGHT:	80kg

ITALY

Caps	133
Goals	0

CLUB CAREER

Games	525
Goals	0
Current club	Juventus

Goalkeeper Buffon shows no sign of hanging up his gloves just yet. The reliable 35 year old signed a contract extension that will see him stay at Juventus – who he has served with distinction since 2001 – until 2015. In truth, Buffon has had busier seasons than 2012-13, his defence forming "an unsinkable ship" (according to Jose Mourinho) in front of him, while in European action he made his 400th Juventus appearance in all competitions in a 2-2 draw against Chelsea. Despite four Serie A titles with the Bianconeri, Buffon's career highlight was the 2006 World Cup triumph with Italy.

SERGIO BUSQUETS

DOB:	16.07.1988
POSITION:	Midfield
HEIGHT:	189cm
WEIGHT:	73kg

SPAIN

Caps	59
Goals	0

CLUB CAREER

Games	170
Goals	6
Current club	FC Barcelona

Football has many unsung heroes and while Barcelona and Spain's flair players receive most of the plaudits, Busquets is truly indispensable. The defensive midfielder's greatest strength is his passing, for he rarely gives the ball away. "He's the first to see the first-time pass, plays with his head up and constantly chooses the best options," enthused team-mate Xavi. His ball control is exemplary while his ability to protect his defence enables players in front of him to attack. In his first five full seasons, Busquets has won the World Cup and European Championship as well as four La Liga titles and the Champions League twice.

EDINSON
CAVANI

DOB:	14.02.1987
POSITION:	Forward
HEIGHT:	184cm
WEIGHT:	71kg

URUGUAY

Caps	54
Goals	17

CLUB CAREER

Games	238
Goals	121
Current club	Paris St Germain

With 29 goals in 34 league matches for Napoli in 2012-13, it is no surprise Cavani was wanted by Europe's elite clubs. The Uruguayan striker bagged four in one game in a Europa League victory against Dnipro Dnipropetrovsk before finishing top scorer in Serie A, six goals ahead of rival Antonio di Natalie, who had beaten him to the feat two seasons previously. Cavani, who scored in Napoli's 2012 Coppa Italia triumph over Juventus, appears to have everything. Agile, powerful and a natural finisher with an aerial presence, Cavani scored three goals in the Confederations Cup before joining French champions PSG.

SANTI CAZORLA

DOB:	**13.12.1984**
POSITION:	**Midfield**
HEIGHT:	**168cm**
WEIGHT:	**66kg**

SPAIN

Caps	56
Goals	9

CLUB CAREER

Games	330
Goals	54
Current club	**Arsenal**

Cazorla signed for Arsenal in the summer of 2012 and filled the void left by compatriot Cesc Fàbregas, who had left for Barcelona a year earlier. The playmaker enjoys a free role behind Arsenal's attackers and has the ability to control games and orchestrate forward play thanks to a combination of incisive passing, intelligent movement and neat close control. He joined from Malaga and settled quickly after winning his second European Championship winners' medal with Spain. By the end of 2012-13, he had scored 12 goals, achieved one of the highest successful pass-completion rates in the league and created almost 100 chances.

GIORGIO CHIELLINI

DOB:	**14.08.1984**
POSITION:	**Defender**
HEIGHT:	**186cm**
WEIGHT:	**76kg**

ITALY

Caps	63
Goals	3

CLUB CAREER

Games	320
Goals	25
Current club	**Juventus**

Chiellini formed part of a Juventus defence that kept 14 clean sheets in their Scudetto-retaining 2012-13 campaign and another four in Europe. The fulcrum of a solid back three, Chiellini is an uncompromising player who leads with robust challenges and constant marshalling of those around him. Three times named Serie A defender if the year, he also boasts a good range of passing, a long throw and crossing ability from wide on the left. Chiellini helped Italy reach the European Championship final in 2012 and his withdrawal after just 20 minutes was seen as the turning point for the Azzurri, who lost 4-0.

ÁNGEL DI MARÍA

DOB:	**14.02.1988**
POSITION:	**Midfield**
HEIGHT:	**178cm**
WEIGHT:	**75kg**

ARGENTINA

Caps	39
Goals	8

CLUB CAREER

Games	200
Goals	31
Current club	**Real Madrid**

Slim in stature but overflowing with pace and skill, Argentina international Di María is an effective attacking player who loves to take on defenders, never stops running and can play wide or behind a central striker. Di María is arguably at his most potent cutting in from the right onto his left foot and Borussia Dortmund coach Jürgen Klopp conceded: "You can't mark him." He rose to prominence at Benfica, who he joined for £5m. Three years later he moved on to Real Madrid for four times that fee and has already won La Liga and the Copa del Rey.

CHRISTIAN ERIKSEN

DOB:	14.02.1992
POSITION:	Midfield
HEIGHT:	175cm
WEIGHT:	65kg

DENMARK

Caps	36
Goals	3

CLUB CAREER

Games	109
Goals	23
Current club	Ajax

Attacking midfielder Eriksen's Ajax performances really caught the eye in 2012/13. Manchester City were on the receiving end of an Eriksen strike in the Champions League and the Citizens were soon rumoured to be among those looking to secure the youngster's services in the summer. He scored 13 goals in all competitions, six shy of his best a year earlier, but he remains influential for club and country. He has won three consecutive league titles with Ajax – the first, in 2010-11, ended the club's seven-year winless streak. Later that summer, Eriksen broke Michael Laudrup's record by becoming the youngest player to score for Denmark in European qualification.

CESC
FÀBREGAS

DOB:	**04.05.1987**
POSITION:	**Midfield**
HEIGHT:	**180cm**
WEIGHT:	**69kg**

SPAIN

Caps	83
Goals	13

CLUB CAREER

Games	272
Goals	55
Current club	**FC Barcelona**

Former Arsenal midfielder Fàbregas rejoined Barcelona – where he spent six years as a trainee – from the London giants in 2011 for £35m. He won his first La Liga title in 2013 shortly after scoring his first hat-trick for the club. This followed success in the Copa del Rey, Supercopa de España, UEFA Super Cup and the FIFA Club World Cup the previous season, during which he scored 15 goals and contributed 20 assists. He has been in and out of the team under Barça boss Tito Vilanova prompting rumours of a Premier League return, but that could change if the Catalans ring the changes this summer.

RADAMEL
FALCAO

DOB:	**10.02.1986**
POSITION:	**Forward**
HEIGHT:	**175cm**
WEIGHT:	**78kg**

COLOMBIA

Caps	46
Goals	17

CLUB CAREER

Games	209
Goals	128
Current club	**AS Monaco**

Monaco fans must be looking forward to seeing prolific Colombian striker Falcao in action following his record £54m deal. The same cannot be said for opposing goalkeepers who will look at his goalscoring record with trepidation – all told he has smashed in an incredible 145 goals in over 260 games for club and country, 70 in 90 for previous club Atlético Madrid alone. He left Madrid on a high after winning his first domestic title with victory against rivals Real Madrid (Atlético's first derby win in 14 years). In 2011–12, Falcao's goals helped Los Rojiblancos to a UEFA Super Cup and Europa League double.

RYAN GIGGS

DOB:	**29.11.1973**
POSITION:	**Midfield**
HEIGHT:	**181cm**
WEIGHT:	**68kg**

WALES

Caps	64
Goals	12

CLUB CAREER

Games	941
Goals	168
Current club	Manchester United

"A unique freak" was how Sir Alex Ferguson described Ryan Giggs, the midfielder with almost 200 more Manchester United appearances to his name than any other player. His 23rd season at Old Trafford, 2012-13, brought the Welshman his 13th Premier League title, his 1,000th senior appearance and a one-year contract extension that will see him play into his 40s. Giggs is a phenomenon – he can still attack with the same vigour that made him football's trickiest winger when he arrived on the scene in 1991. Now using his experience in a deeper role, the one-club man has 34 winners' medals and counting.

MARIO GÖTZE

DOB:	03.06.1992
POSITION:	Midfield
HEIGHT:	176cm
WEIGHT:	64kg

GERMANY

Caps	22
Goals	5

CLUB CAREER

Games	83
Goals	22
Current club	Bayern Munich

The 2013 Champions League final must have been an odd occasion for a player many consider the future of German football. Attacking midfielder Götze helped Borussia Dortmund reach the Wembley showpiece with his vision and skill, but sat in the stands as his new team-mates [he joins Bayern Munich for £31.5m] lifted the trophy. Dubbed "the Lionel Messi of Germany" by Franz Beckenbauer, Götze becomes the country's most expensive player. The 20-year-old was born in Bavaria and used to have Bayern bedsheets, according to coach Helmut Albat. But he helped Dortmund win consecutive league titles in 2011 and 2012 before his controversial switch.

MAREK HAMŠÍK

DOB:	**27.07.1987**
POSITION:	**Midfield**
HEIGHT:	**170cm**
WEIGHT:	**69kg**

SLOVAKIA

Caps	64
Goals	10

CLUB CAREER

Games	284
Goals	72
Current club	**SSC Napoli**

A cult icon for his playmaking and passing abilities, Slovakian international Hamšík is one of the most dangerous midfielders in Serie A. Played on the right in his younger days, in 2013 he was deployed in a more central role and responded with 13 assists – four more than any other player in the division. Hamšík is at his most dangerous when spraying the ball into wide positions or carving open opposing defences. In 2010-11 he helped Napoli qualify for the Champions League before lifting the Coppa Italia in 2012 – the club's first silverware for 22 years.

EDEN
HAZARD

DOB:	**07.01.1991**
POSITION:	**Midfield**
HEIGHT:	**170cm**
WEIGHT:	**69kg**

BELGIUM

Caps	37
Goals	5

CLUB CAREER

Games	181
Goals	45
Current club	**Chelsea**

Belgian playmaker Hazard is a dangerous attacking midfielder whose reputation has been enhanced following his move to Chelsea in 2012 after a four-year spell at French side Lille. The first player since Zinedine Zidane to win the French Player of the Year award twice, Hazard won the French league and cup double with Lille and has since settled well in London, his dribbling ability, trickery and pace helping his new team finish third in the Premier League and win the Europa League. Hazard can play in the middle or wide and he has enjoyed particular success cutting in from the left.

XAVI
HERNÁNDEZ

DOB:	**25.01.1980**
POSITION:	**Midfielder**
HEIGHT:	**170cm**
WEIGHT:	**66kg**

SPAIN

Caps	126
Goals	11

CLUB CAREER

Games	505
Goals	57
Current club	**FC Barcelona**

Stylish Spaniard Xavi has been the fulcrum of Barcelona's midfield for a decade, producing accomplished performances week after week to secure him every honour in the game. The compact midfielder broke into the Barça first team in 1998-99 in a deep-lying position. Now, he plays further forward in a free role that allows him to pull the strings, displaying an almost telepathic understanding with Andrés Iniesta and Lionel Messi. One of the game's great passers, Xavi does not concede possession lightly. Spain's most-capped outfield player, he has played an integral role in the recent Barça-dominated era of European football.

HULK

DOB:	25.07.1986
POSITION:	Forward
HEIGHT:	178cm
WEIGHT:	68kg

BRAZIL

Caps	27
Goals	6

CLUB CAREER

Games	221
Goals	131
Current club	Zenit St Petersburg

The Brazilian striker spent 2012-13 in Russia, but the clamour for the barrel-chested striker to join one of Europe's major leagues continues to grow. A dangerous forward, Hulk's goals helped previous club FC Porto win ten major titles, including the Europa League in 2011. He finished top scorer in the Primeira Liga that year and his consistency persuaded Zenit St Petersburg to part with £34.1m for his services. Despite seven goals in 18 games, Hulk has failed to settle in Russia, prompting rumours of a move.

MATS
HUMMELS

DOB:	16.12.1988
POSITION:	Defender
HEIGHT:	191cm
WEIGHT:	88kg

GERMANY

Caps	24
Goals	1

CLUB CAREER

Games	191
Goals	18
Current club	Borussia Dortmund

Hummels was just eight years old when Borussia Dortmund won the Champions League in 1997. Sixteen years later, the consistent defender was a key player as Die Borussen reached the final to face Bayern Munich, the club he supported as a boy. Centre-back Hummels scored a crucial equaliser against Shakhtar Donetsk in the last 16 and won 20 of his 24 challenges against Real Madrid in the semi-final. The two-time league winner and German international won two-thirds of his challenges in all competitions last season. He is strong in the air, boasts excellent positional sense and can start attacks from defence.

KLAAS-JAN
HUNTELAAR

DOB:	12.08.1983
POSITION:	Forward
HEIGHT:	186cm
WEIGHT:	80kg

NETHERLANDS

Caps	59
Goals	34

CLUB CAREER

Games	306
Goals	195
Current club	FC Schalke 04

Prolific striker Huntelaar is in a rich vein of form. In 2012-13, he scored ten goals in 25 Bundesliga matches, four in six European games and four in five internationals for the Netherlands. The previous season, 'Hunter' scored 47 in 52 matches in all competitions for club and country – and 24 in 37 the season before that ... you get the picture. Huntelaar rose to prominence on loan at AGOVV Apeldoorn, who named a stand after him, before netting 17 goals in his first full Eredivisie campaign with Heerenveen. His goal-getting prompted moves to Ajax, AC Milan and Real Madrid before a 2010 switch to Schalke.

ZLATAN
IBRAHIMOVIĆ

DOB:	**03.10.1981**
POSITION:	**Forward**
HEIGHT:	**192cm**
WEIGHT:	**84kg**

SWEDEN

Caps	90
Goals	41

CLUB CAREER

Games	396
Goals	219
Current club	**Paris St Germain**

Skilful Swede Ibrahimović offers current employers Paris St Germain a range of attacking options. His height and strength enable him to lead the line and retain possession, but he can also drop deeper into the space between midfield and attack to create chances. Wherever he plays, Ibrahimović guarantees goals and silverware. He has won 11 domestic titles in 13 seasons, most recently a Ligue 1 title with PSG in 2013, their first for 19 years. In the same season, he became the first player to score for six different clubs in the Champions League and stunned the world with a spectacular long-range overhead kick against England.

ANDRÉS INIESTA

DOB:	**11.05.1984**
POSITION:	**Midfield**
HEIGHT:	**170cm**
WEIGHT:	**72kg**

SPAIN

Caps	87
Goals	11

CLUB CAREER

Games	351
Goals	36
Current club	**FC Barcelona**

The dominance of Barcelona and Spain in the last decade owes much to the brilliance and genius of Iniesta. Described as "the complete player" by Louis van Gaal, the man who gave him his Barça debut in 2002, Iniesta has been an instrumental force behind the Catalan giants' six La Liga titles and three Champions League triumphs since 2004. Nicknamed 'The Brain', he starts and finishes attacks, his movement and range of passing a vital weapon when it comes to unlocking defences. He scores important goals, too – none more so than the dramatic late winner in the 2010 World Cup final for Spain.

BRANISLAV
IVANOVIC

DOB:	**22.02.1984**
POSITION:	**Defender**
HEIGHT:	**188cm**
WEIGHT:	**84kg**

SERBIA

Caps	60
Goals	7

CLUB CAREER

Games	250
Goals	23
Current club	Chelsea

Quiet defender Ivanovic surprised everyone when he clambered onto the crossbar to celebrate Chelsea's Europa League success in May, the Serbian having scored a dramatic late winner. Yet Ivanovic had good reason to celebrate, for the powerful and commanding defender had enjoyed an exceptional season. He scored nine goals in all competitions in 2012-13, his winner against Benfica in Amsterdam arguably the most important. It was his ninth for the club in European action – and his Europa League winners' medal now sits proudly alongside those for winning the Champions League, Premier League and FA Cup.

VINCENT KOMPANY

DOB:	10.04.1986
POSITION:	Defender
HEIGHT:	190cm
WEIGHT:	85kg

BELGIUM

Caps	54
Goals	4

CLUB CAREER

Games	255
Goals	13
Current club	Manchester City

Described by team-mate Jack Rodwell as "one of the best centre-halves in the world," Kompany's importance to Manchester City is perhaps best highlighted by the team's disappointing form when he was sidelined with a calf injury in 2012-13, dropping ten points, which seriously damaged their chances of retaining the Premier League title. After starting his career in midfield, Kompany has evolved into a quick defender with excellent positioning, presence and the ability to make crucial interventions. The towering 27-year-old combines strength in the air with confidence in possession and is captain of the highly-rated Belgian national team.

TONI KROOS

DOB:	04.01.1990
POSITION:	Midfield
HEIGHT:	180cm
WEIGHT:	77kg

GERMANY

Caps	35
Goals	4

CLUB CAREER

Games	157
Goals	25
Current club	Bayern Munich

Young German midfielder Kroos is a versatile, dynamic and hard-working creative playmaker equally as adept surging forward and creating chances as breaking up play and closing opponents down. Practically ever-present until a knee injury against Juventus in the Champions League quarter-final cut his season short, Kroos's 2012-13 statistics were phenomenal, with an average pass success rate of almost 90 per cent – remarkable when you consider most of his contributions were made in the final third. He contributed eight assists and scored nine goals as he helped Bayern Munich on the road to long-awaited European glory.

PHILIP
LAHM

DOB:	11.11.1983
POSITION:	Defender
HEIGHT:	170cm
WEIGHT:	65kg

GERMANY

Caps	98
Goals	5

CLUB CAREER

Games	349
Goals	12
Current club	Bayern Munich

Few players can match Lahm's athleticism and consistency. Captain for hometown club and country, the 29-year-old won his fifth Bundesliga winners' medal before lifting the Champions League trophy at the third time of asking and the German Cup a week later in May. Lahm was key to Bayern's success – in Bundesliga action, no player touched the ball more while in Europe he played more minutes than any of his outfield team-mates. He created five goals (only Bastien Schweinsteiger and Zlatan Ibrahimović made more assists), was second only to Barcelona's Dani Alves with crosses delivered and won two-thirds of his tackles.

FRANK LAMPARD

DOB:	20.06.1978
POSITION:	Midfielder
HEIGHT:	182cm
WEIGHT:	88kg

ENGLAND

Caps	97
Goals	29

CLUB CAREER

Games	805
Goals	227
Current club	Chelsea

ENGLAND

Box-to-box midfielder Lampard overtook Bobby Tambling's record of 202 goals in all competitions to become Chelsea's highest scorer of all time in May 2013. Lampard was out of contract when he achieved the feat, but he went on to lift the Europa League following Chelsea's last-gasp 2-1 win against Benfica in Amsterdam to add to his collection of three league titles, four FA Cups and one Champions League winners' medal – and earn a new one-year deal. The fourth highest goalscorer in Premier League history, Lampard is also England's most prolific midfielder ever with 29 international goals.

ROBERT
LEWANDOWSKI

DOB:	**21.08.1988**
POSITION:	**Forward**
HEIGHT:	**181cm**
WEIGHT:	**71kg**

POLAND

Caps	54
Goals	17

CLUB CAREER

Games	225
Goals	126
Current club	**Borussia Dortmund**

Strong Polish striker Lewandowski has become one of football's hottest properties following an impressive 2012–13 campaign. The 24-year-old showed all of his predatory instincts with a remarkable 34-goal haul, ten of which came in the Champions League. He scored four during one particular virtuoso performance, against Real Madrid in the first leg of the semi-finals, making him the first player to strike four times at that stage of the competition. His goalscoring ability is enhanced by his upper-body strength and ability with his back to goal. Lewandowski has already won two Bundesliga titles and scored 17 goals for his country.

FERNANDO LLORENTE

DOB:	26.02.1985
POSITION:	Forward
HEIGHT:	193cm
WEIGHT:	88kg

SPAIN

Caps	21
Goals	7

CLUB CAREER

Games	311
Goals	101
Current club	Juventus

Bad news for Serie A goalkeepers next season – not content with winning consecutive titles, Juventus have strengthened further with the signing of unsettled Spanish striker Fernando Llorente. The 28-year-old switches to Turin from Athletic Bilbao in a move that will have disappointed a number of English teams keen on securing his services. Llorente spent nine seasons at Bilbao after graduating from their academy and scored 101 goals in 334 appearances in all competitions. But after falling out with the management, he was used as an impact substitute in his final season, making 22 of his 26 La Liga appearances from the bench.

CLAUDIO
MARCHISIO

DOB:	19.01.1986
POSITION:	Midfield
HEIGHT:	180cm
WEIGHT:	70kg

ITALY

Caps	38
Goals	2

CLUB CAREER

Games	200
Goals	25
Current club	Juventus

Juventus boasted an embarrassment of riches in midfield during 2012–13, with versatile midfielder Claudio Marchisio one of the most impressive and consistent performers. A box-to-box player who works tirelessly to protect his back four, the 27-year-old also scored six league goals as his side clinched a second consecutive Scudetto and enjoyed a run to the quarter-finals in the Champions League. He made his breakthrough in Turin under Claudio Ranieri in 2007–08 and reached his century of appearances midway through the 2011–12 campaign. That summer, Marchisio played every minute of every game as Italy reached the Euro 2012 final.

JUAN
MATA

DOB:	28.04.1988
POSITION:	Midfield
HEIGHT:	175cm
WEIGHT:	63kg

SPAIN

Caps	29
Goals	8

CLUB CAREER

Games	237
Goals	60
Current club	Chelsea

Days after lifting the Europa League trophy in Amsterdam in May, 12 months on from Chelsea's Champions League triumph – diminutive Spanish midfielder Juan Mata was awarded the club's Player of the Year award for the second season in a row. The playmaker scored 20 goals and contributed 27 assists in all competitions and became only the fourth man in the club's history to win the award in consecutive seasons after John Hollins, Ray Wilkins and Frank Lampard. The former Valencia star also lifted the FA Cup in 2012 but is yet to win a Premier League title with the Blues.

LIONEL MESSI

DOB:	24.06.1987
POSITION:	Forward
HEIGHT:	169cm
WEIGHT:	67kg

ARGENTINA

Caps	81
Goals	32

CLUB CAREER

Games	276
Goals	226
Current club	FC Barcelona

The finest player of his generation, Messi has been described by his Barcelona team-mates as "irreplaceable" and it's easy to see why. In January 2013, the Argentina striker won the Ballon d'Or for a record fourth time. In February he scored his 300th Barcelona goal and a month later he became the first player to score against every other team in La Liga in 19 consecutive matches. In 2011–12, he scored a record-breaking 73 goals; 50 in the league and 14 in the Champions League, both separate records and rattled in eight La Liga hat-tricks – all at the age of just 24.

THOMAS MÜLLER

DOB:	13.09.1989
POSITION:	Midfield
HEIGHT:	186cm
WEIGHT:	74kg

GERMANY

Caps	41
Goals	13

CLUB CAREER

Games	170
Goals	62
Current club	**Bayern Munich**

Thomas Müller had good reason to enjoy the climax of the 2012–13 season. The intelligent and composed attacking midfielder helped Bayern Munich secure the Bundesliga title before lifting the Champions League trophy in May and scoring in the German Cup final victory against Stuttgart. It was a proud treble for a player who climbed the club's ranks before making his professional debut in 2008. Remembered by England supporters for his brace in Germany's 4-1 victory at the 2010 World Cup, the player who averages a goal every three games for club and country recently signed an extended deal to keep him at the Allianz Arena until 2017.

MANUEL NEUER

DOB:	**27.03.1986**
POSITION:	**Goalkeeper**
HEIGHT:	**192cm**
WEIGHT:	**85kg**

GERMANY

Caps	38
Goals	0

CLUB CAREER

Games	247
Goals	0
Current club	**Bayern Munich**

Impressive shot-stopping skills, astonishing reflexes and an ability to create attacks with long throws – think former Manchester United stopper Peter Schmeichel at his peak – make Bayern Munich No.1 Neuer one of world football's most talented goalkeepers. The late developer once considered too small now boasts a huge presence between the posts. He joined current club Bayern from Schalke in 2011 in a deal that made him the second most expensive goalkeeper in the world behind Italian legend Gianluigi Buffon. In 2012–13, he shone as Bayern won an impressive Bundesliga, Champions League and German Cup treble.

NEYMAR

DOB:	05.02.1992
POSITION:	Forward
HEIGHT:	174cm
WEIGHT:	65kg

BRAZIL

Caps	39
Goals	24

CLUB CAREER

Games	103
Goals	53
Current club	FC Barcelona

Pele suggests Neymar "could be better than me", which should set expectation levels high for Barcelona fans. Their new Brazilian signing plays predominantly as a second striker – centrally or as an inside forward cutting in from the left – but he can also play in a deeper role. Twice voted South American Footballer of the Year, in 2011 Neymar helped Santos lift the Copa Libertadores – and the following season he scored 43 goals in 47 games as they clinched their third consecutive Brazilian title. Neymar was the star attraction with four goals as Brazil won the Confederations Cup on home soil in the summer.

MESUT ÖZIL

DOB:	**15.10.1988**
POSITION:	**Forward**
HEIGHT:	**180cm**
WEIGHT:	**70kg**

GERMANY

Caps	46
Goals	14

CLUB CAREER

Games	204
Goals	32
Current club	**Real Madrid**

German playmaker Özil was recently described by departing Real Madrid boss Jose Mourinho as the "best No10 in the world," and despite a modest frame, the 24-year-old has the ability to dominate for club and country from midfield. Gelsenkirchen-born Özil is creative but just as likely to be making a key tackle or interception as pulling a player out of position or executing a killer pass in the final third. The former Schalke and Werder Bremen star created the most goals for Madrid in Europe last season and his tireless performances make him an essential part of their engine room.

GERARD
PIQUÉ

DOB:	**02.02.1987**
POSITION:	**Defender**
HEIGHT:	**185cm**
WEIGHT:	**75kg**

SPAIN

Caps	57
Goals	4

CLUB CAREER

Games	172
Goals	12
Current club	**FC Barcelona**

The look on Piqué's face following Barcelona's capitulation in the Champions League semi-final at the hands of Bayern Munich said it all; this is a player not used to losing games. It was a rare bitter pill to swallow for the commanding 26-year-old defender, who has already won more trophies than most players dream of – Barça's La Liga triumph in 2012–13, with 100 points – was his fourth since returning to the club in 2008 from Manchester United. He has also won three Champions Leagues and three domestic cups, not to mention a World cup and European Championship double with Spain.

ANDREA PIRLO

DOB:	19.05.1979
POSITION:	Midfield
HEIGHT:	175cm
WEIGHT:	67kg

ITALY

Caps	102
Goals	13

CLUB CAREER

Games	460
Goals	52
Current club	Juventus

Described as "embarrassingly good" by team-mate Gianluigi Buffon and "the strongest midfielder in the world" by former manager Carlo Ancelotti, classy midfielder Pirlo appears to be getting better with age. When he left AC Milan for Juventus aged 32 in 2011 many thought his best days were behind him, yet 'The Architect' helped steer the Bianconeri to consecutive Serie A titles in 2012 and 2013. A deep-lying playmaker with unerring accuracy, vision and passing, Pirlo had already won two Scudettos with Milan before the recent double. A losing finalist with Italy, he was one of the outstanding players at Euro 2012.

SERGIO
RAMOS

DOB:	30.03.1986
POSITION:	Defender
HEIGHT:	183cm
WEIGHT:	73kg

SPAIN

Caps	108
Goals	9

CLUB CAREER

Games	319
Goals	36
Current club	Real Madrid

Sergio Ramos is a skilful and committed defender (he has a tattoo that reads Unconquerable Soul) with almost every footballing honour to his name - only the Champions League eludes him. He won the World Cup with Spain in 2010 and was part of the squad that won consecutive European Championships in 2008 and 2012. He has also won three La Liga titles and a Copa del Rey with Real Madrid, the club he has represented – first as right-back, now centre-back – for eight seasons. He has vast experience, reads the game well and is accomplished with the ball at his feet.

MARCO
REUS

DOB:	31.05.1989
POSITION:	Midfield
HEIGHT:	180cm
WEIGHT:	67kg

GERMANY

Caps	15
Goals	7

CLUB CAREER

Games	165
Goals	52
Current club	Borussia Dortmund

Borussia Dortmund's disappointment at losing Shinji Kagawa to Manchester United in 2012 quickly evaporated with the return of Marco Reus. The 23-year-old had been part of Dortmund's youth set-up but rose to prominence at Borussia Mönchengladbach, where he scored 18 league goals in his final season. Back at Dortmund, Reus has delivered a number of eye-catching performances, particularly in Europe, where his dangerous right foot, technique and trickery have proved too much for defenders. Increasingly valuable to the national team, Reus scored on his first competitive start for Germany, against Greece in the Euro 2012 quarter-finals.

FRANCK
RIBÉRY

DOB:	01.04.1983
POSITION:	Midfield
HEIGHT:	170cm
WEIGHT:	62kg

FRANCE

Caps	73
Goals	12

CLUB CAREER

Games	324
Goals	74
Current club	Bayern Munich

A talented and experienced wide player who Bayern Munich president Franz Beckenbauer believes is "worth a comparable sum" to Cristiano Ronaldo, Ribéry showcased his talents with a stunning finish on the final day of the 2012–13 domestic season. The Frenchman volleyed home from the edge of the area to salvage a point for the new Bundesliga champions. Two weeks later, he lifted the Champions League trophy before winning a German Cup winner's medal. Although he had never spent more than two seasons at any of his six previous clubs before joining Bayern in 2007, scoring spectacular goals is nothing new for Ribéry.

ARJEN ROBBEN

DOB:	23.01.1984
POSITION:	Midfield
HEIGHT:	180cm
WEIGHT:	75kg

NETHERLANDS

Caps	68
Goals	18

CLUB CAREER

Games	298
Goals	96
Current club	Bayern Munich

KNVB®

Scoring the decisive late goal in the 2013 Champions League final completed a remarkable turnaround for Dutch winger Robben, who has been terrorising full-backs for 13 years. The 29-year-old's winner came 12 months after missing a penalty against former club Chelsea in the 2012 showpiece. Practically one-footed, the Dutchman loves to take on defenders and cross or shoot with his favoured left boot, but he faced fierce competition for a starting place for much of 2012-13. Fourteen Bayern players enjoyed more league minutes than Robben last season – although his man-of-the-match performance in London put him firmly back on the radar.

JAMES
RODRÍGUEZ

DOB:	**12.07.1991**
POSITION:	**Midfield**
HEIGHT:	**178cm**
WEIGHT:	**78kg**

COLOMBIA

Caps	13
Goals	2

CLUB CAREER

Games	107
Goals	30
Current club	**AS Monaco**

Rising star Rodríguez was coveted by a number of clubs before his £38.5m transfer to rising French force Monaco. The playmaker's form for FC Porto has drawn comparisons with Colombian legend Carlos Valderrama. The hair is different and Rodríguez is left-footed, not right - but he wears Colombia's famous No10 shirt and has the potential to become as pivotal as his famous predecessor. Rodriguez joined Porto in July 2010 and has contributed 28 goals – and many assists – from central or wide-left positions. His form has helped the club win two league titles, a Portuguese Cup, two Portuguese Supercups and the Europa League.

CRISTIANO
RONALDO

DOB:	**05.02.1985**
POSITION:	**Forward**
HEIGHT:	**184cm**
WEIGHT:	**75kg**

PORTUGAL

Caps	104
Goals	38

CLUB CAREER

Games	356
Goals	233
Current club	**Real Madrid**

Ronaldo's statistics make for breathtaking reading. In 2012-13 the attacker described by Sir Alex Ferguson as "the complete player" scored 54 goals in 54 appearances, including five hat-tricks. It took his tally since joining Real Madrid to 206 goals in 195 games, making him the third-highest scorer in their history. In 2011-12, Ronaldo set a new club mark for individual goals scored in one year with 60 and became the first player ever to score against all 19 opposing teams in one season. Sold by Manchester United in 2009 for £80m, Ronaldo is still the most expensive player in history.

WAYNE ROONEY

DOB:	24.10.1985
POSITION:	Forward
HEIGHT:	177cm
WEIGHT:	78kg

ENGLAND

Caps	83
Goals	36

CLUB CAREER

Games	345
Goals	156
Current club	Manchester United

ENGLAND

The tenacious forward signed off 2012/13 with a stunning goal for England against Brazil in the revamped Maracanã and his unique, swashbuckling style of play continues to make him a goalscoring threat. He provided 12 league goals and ten assists before picking up his fifth Premier League title with United since joining the club from Everton in 2004. Overall, he has surpassed the 20-goal mark in four out of seven seasons at Old Trafford. Whether leading the attack, playing wide or in a subdued role, Rooney always gives his all. He has great vision, a tremendous work rate and powerful build.

BASTIAN
SCHWEINSTEIGER

DOB:	01.08.1984
POSITION:	Midfield
HEIGHT:	180cm
WEIGHT:	76kg

GERMANY

Caps	98
Goals	23

CLUB CAREER

Games	330
Goals	38
Current club	Bayern Munich

When Bayern Munich vice-captain Schweinsteiger lifted the German Cup in May he equalled Oliver Kahn's record of six winners' medals in the competition. The Cup win was the last piece of a remarkable redemption for a player who joined the club aged 13. Twelve months previously, Schweinsteiger missed the pivotal spot-kick that saw Bayern lose the 2012 final on their home ground against Chelsea. The 28-year-old midfielder was distraught but later admitted the experience was "added motivation" as he played a key role when Die Bayern went one better at Wembley.

STEPHAN EL SHAARAWY

DOB:	27.10.1992
POSITION:	Forward
HEIGHT:	180cm
WEIGHT:	70kg

ITALY

Caps	8
Goals	1

CLUB CAREER

Games	87
Goals	25
Current club	AC Milan

Arguably the best thing to have come out of AC Milan's transitional summer in 2011 was the arrival of striker Stephan El Shaarawy. Brought in as a potential replacement for Zlatan Ibrahimović the following summer, Shaarawy is now one of the hottest prospects in Italian football. Comfortable with the ball at his feet, Shaarawy – who sports an iconic mohican haircut – can play in attack or in midfield. He has the ability to take players on and is dangerous in front of goal, netting 18 times in all competitions in 2012-13. The youngster made his full international debut against England last summer.

DAVID
SILVA

DOB:	**08.01.1986**
POSITION:	**Midfield**
HEIGHT:	**172cm**
WEIGHT:	**67kg**

SPAIN

Caps	75
Goals	20

CLUB CAREER

Games	305
Goals	44
Current club	**Manchester City**

Like so many Spanish midfielders, Manchester City star Silva is small in size but big in ability and at times the ball seems stuck to his foot, such is his close control. Signed from financially-troubled Valencia, with whom he won the 2008 Copa del Rey, Silva was an instant hit at the Etihad. Since arriving in 2011, he has played a major part in the club's success, providing 15 assists as they won the league in 2011-12 - his ability to find team-mates with passes at times defying logic. That summer, he provided three assists as Spain retained the European Championship.

THIAGO
SILVA

DOB:	22.09.1984
POSITION:	Defender
HEIGHT:	183cm
WEIGHT:	79kg

BRAZIL

Caps	40
Goals	1

CLUB CAREER

Games	223
Goals	14
Current club	Paris St Germain

Brazil is more famed for producing exciting attacking players than defenders, but skipper Thiago Silva is considered one of the best in Europe. He joined Paris St Germain in 2012 and was reunited with Zlatan Ibrahimović, the duo having played at AC Milan. Thiago's sensational pace, leadership and strength in the air were a key factor in Carlo Ancelotti's side winning the Ligue 1 title. Thiago has certainly added steel to the Parisiens' back line, the Brazilian reproducing the kind of form that saw the Rossoneri enjoy 33 clean sheets in his last two seasons in Italy.

LUIS SUÀREZ

DOB:	24/01/1987
POSITION:	Forward
HEIGHT:	181cm
WEIGHT:	81kg

URUGUAY

Caps	69
Goals	35

CLUB CAREER

Games	243
Goals	139
Current club	Liverpool

Controversy is never far from this enigmatic Uruguayan centre-forward, but there is no denying Suàrez was one of the most consistent Premier League players in 2012–13. He scored 30 goals in 44 games for Liverpool, including two hat-tricks, and 11 in 15 for Uruguay. Reds skipper Steven Gerrard insists he is the best player he has ever played alongside - the 29-year-old spearheaded Liverpool's attack with aplomb, at times on his own. But frighteningly, Suàrez's figures could be even better – currently serving a ten-match ban, ill-discipline has caused him to miss 26 games through suspension since arriving on Merseyside

CARLOS TÉVEZ

DOB:	**05.02.1984**
POSITION:	**Forward**
HEIGHT:	**173cm**
WEIGHT:	**74kg**

ARGENTINA

Caps	64
Goals	13

CLUB CAREER

Games	315
Goals	134
Current club	**Juventus**

Premier League defenders will be pleased to see the back of the industrious Tévez who recently swapped Manchester City for Juventus after scoring 79 goals in four seasons. Last season, he returned to his best after a disappointing 2011-12 campaign sullied by a row with the club's management. Tévez lit up 2013 with eight goals in a nine-game spell, his low centre of gravity, pace and ability to create shooting opportunities in small spaces causing havoc. Tévez joined City from Manchester rivals United in 2009, having scored 34 goals in 99 games for the Reds and lifted the Champions League and two Premier League titles.

YAYA TOURÉ

DOB:	**13.05.1983**
POSITION:	**Midfield**
HEIGHT:	**187cm**
WEIGHT:	**78kg**

IVORY COAST

Caps	74
Goals	14

CLUB CAREER

Games	323
Goals	38
Current club	**Manchester City**

When powerful Manchester City and Ivory Coast midfielder Yaya Touré is at his best he is simply unplayable. As former City manager Roberto Mancini explained: "He is strong, quick, has good technique and can play in different positions." Touré is most deadly when rampaging through midfield, his tremendous pace and powerful frame difficult to defend against. The Ivorian scored the winning goal when City lifted the FA Cup in 2011, then provided the driving force behind their Premier League success the following season, adding to the two La Liga winners' medals picked up during a glittering three-year spell at Barcelona.

VICTOR
VALDÉS

DOB:	14.01.1982
POSITION:	Goalkeeper
HEIGHT:	186cm
WEIGHT:	76kg

SPAIN

Caps	15
Goals	0

CLUB CAREER

Games	438
Goals	0
Current club	FC Barcelona

Victor Valdés and Barcelona have been a perfect match for 11 years and the Spanish goalkeeper has delayed moving on until 2014, when his current contract runs out at Camp Nou. Valdés will be a valuable addition wherever he goes next year, combining excellent shot-stopping skills and concentration – often after long spells without anything to do – with confidence on the ball. "He wins you a lot of points," insisted compatriot Gerard Piqué. Valdés also wins a lot of medals – the 2012–13 La Liga title was his sixth league success, while he has also lifted the Champions League trophy three times and the Copa del Rey twice.

ROBIN
VAN PERSIE

DOB:	06.08.1983
POSITION:	Forward
HEIGHT:	182cm
WEIGHT:	69kg

NETHERLANDS

Caps	76
Goals	35

CLUB CAREER

Games	293
Goals	136
Current club	Manchester United

KNVB®

When left-footed striker Van Persie arrived in Manchester in the summer of 2012, former United manager Sir Alex Ferguson claimed the Dutchman was "the finished article". The Scot signed Footballer of the Year Van Persie from under the noses of cross-city rivals Manchester City - and his new recruit's 26 goals arguably proved the difference between the two clubs in the 2012-13 Premier League title race. United's 20th top-flight title brought Van Persie's first league winners' medal after just one FA Cup triumph in eight years at Arsenal, for whom he made 194 Premier League appearances and scored 96 goals.

RAPHAËL VARANE

DOB:	**25.04.1993**
POSITION:	**Defender**
HEIGHT:	**190cm**
WEIGHT:	**85kg**

FRANCE

Caps	2
Goals	0

CLUB CAREER

Games	56
Goals	3
Current club	**Real Madrid**

What a season for rising star Varane, described as "Real Madrid's Lion" by one Spanish newspaper. The 20-year-old centre-back impressed when drafted in as injury cover in 2012-13. In January, against rivals Barcelona, he won the man of the match award and became the second-youngest foreign player to score in El Clásico. His performances belied his age and he ended the campaign a first-choice selection, one of Los Blancos' most consistent performers. He boasts great strength, power, speed and an extraordinary ability to read the game. His technique has drawn comparisons with Madrid legend Fernando Hierro.

MARCO VERRATTI

DOB:	**05.11.1992**
POSITION:	**Midfield**
HEIGHT:	**165cm**
WEIGHT:	**60kg**

ITALY

Caps	3
Goals	1

CLUB CAREER

Games	101
Goals	2
Current club	**Paris St Germain**

ITALIA
FIGC

Midfielder Marco Verratti is a crucial part of Paris St Germain's future after impressing in his first season in the French capital. The deep-lying Italian's greatest asset is protecting his defence and closing down the opposition, best highlighted in PSG's Champions League clash with Barcelona at the Nou Camp, when Verratti came of age. He not only looked comfortable when tracking the best midfield combination in the world, he dictated the play. An aggressive player, Verratti will be unstoppable if he manages to eradicate a propensity to foul, having picked up 23 bookings and three red cards in his last two league campaigns.

ARTURO VIDAL

DOB:	22.05.87
POSITION:	Midfielder
HEIGHT:	181cm
WEIGHT:	75kg

CHILE

Caps	47
Goals	6

CLUB CAREER

Games	211
Goals	34
Current club	Juventus

Combative Chilean midfielder Arturo Vidal's penalty against Palermo in April secured Juventus a 29th Serie A title. It was the 26-year-old's tenth league goal of a memorable 2012–13 campaign and saw him finish as the Bianconeri's top scorer with 14 in all competitions – as well as contributing seven assists. Vidal's attacking capabilities compliment an aggressive box-to-box style. His arrival in Turin in 2011 has coincided with back-to-back Scudettos and a run of form that has seen The Old Lady lose just five of their last 76 league matches. In 2011–12 he made more tackles and more runs than any other player in the Italian top flight.

JACK
WILSHERE

DOB:	01.01.1992
POSITION:	Midfielder
HEIGHT:	170cm
WEIGHT:	64kg

ENGLAND

Caps	7
Goals	0

CLUB CAREER

Games	76
Goals	2
Current club	Arsenal

ENGLAND

The young Arsenal midfielder is touted as a future leader for club and country and two career highlights suggest why. Firstly, his performance against Barcelona in 2011, when he beat midfield duo Xavi and Iniesta at their own game with his own interpretation of 'tika-taka'. Then, in a friendly against Brazil in 2012, he displayed more skill and flair than his Samba opponents, looking particularly impressive when breaking forward with the ball at his feet. He can operate as a deep-lying midfielder linking defence with attack or as a No10 behind his attackers. The biggest challenge facing Wilshere is staying fit.